Speaking for CHANGE

Julie Ellis

Speaking for Change

Text: Julie Ellis
Publishers: Tania Mazzeo and Eliza Webb
Series consultant: Amanda Sutera
Hands on Heads Consulting
Editor: Jess Mackay
Project editor: Annabel Smith
Designer: Leigh Ashforth
Project designer: Danielle Maccarone
Permissions researchers: Lumina Datamatics
Production controller: Renee Tome

Acknowledgements
We would like to thank the following for permission to reproduce copyright material:

Front cover: iStock.com/FabrikaCr; pp. 10, 4 (left); 26 (second from left); backcover: PD Archive/Alamy Stock Photo; pp. 4 (right), 27 (fourth from left) ZUMA Press, Inc./Alamy Stock Photo; p. 5: (left) MediaPunch Inc/Alamy Stock Photo; (right), p.14, p.26 (right) Andrew Sheargold/Getty Images News/Getty Images; p. 7: Carlo Bollo/Alamy Stock Photo; cover; p. 8 (bottom): Hulton Deutsch/Corbis Historical/Getty Images; (top and middle quotes) Emmeline Pankhurst (1913); p. 9: World History Archive/Alamy Stock Photo; p. 11: (top quote) Mahatma Gandhi (1942); (bottom) Anadolu/Getty Image; pp. 12; 26 (third from left): MANUEL CENETA/AFP/Getty Images; p. 13: (top and middle quotes) Whakahuihui Vercoe (1990); (bottom) Tim Graham/Tim Graham Photo Library/Getty Images; p. 15: (top quote) Kevin Rudd (2008); (bottom) Lisa Maree Williams/Getty Images News/Getty Images; pp. 16, 27(left): AAP Image/Lukas Coch; p. 17: (top quote) Julia Gillard (2012); (bottom) AAP Image/Alan Porritt; pp. 18, 27(second from left): STAN HONDA/AFP/Getty Images; p. 19: (top quote) Malala Yousafzai (2013); (bottom) Chirawan Thaiprasansap/Shutterstock.com; pp. 20, 27(third from left): imageBROKER.com GmbH & Co. KG/Alamy Stock Photo; p. 21: (top quote) Jane Goodall (2017); (bottom) CBS Photo Archive/CBS/Getty Images; p. 22: (top)dpa picture alliance/Alamy Stock Photo; (bottom quote) Greta Thunberg (2019); p. 23: (left quote) Greta Thunberg (2019); (right) Steven May/Alamy Stock Photo; pp. 24, 27 (right): Patrick Semansky/UPI/Alamy Stock Photo; p. 25: dpa picture alliance/Alamy Stock Photo; p. 27: LARS HAGBERG/AFP/Getty Images; p. 28: (left) Tommaso Boddi/Getty Images Entertainment/Getty Images; (right) PA Images/Alamy Stock Photo; p. 30: Pixel-Shot/Shutterstock.com.

NovaStar

ISBN 978 0 17 033518 8

Cengage Learning Australia
Level 5, 80 Dorcas Street
Southbank VIC 3006 Australia
Phone: 1300 790 853
Email: aust.nelsonprimary@cengage.com

For learning solutions, visit **cengage.com.au**

Printed in China by 1010 Printing International Ltd
1 2 3 4 5 6 7 29 28 27 26 25

Nelson acknowledges the Traditional Owners and Custodians of the lands of all First Nations Peoples. We pay respect to Elders past and present, and extend that respect to all First Nations Peoples today.

Contents

THE POWER OF WORDS

A speech is when one person talks and other people listen. The speaker may share ideas, tell stories, explain something or express how they feel about a topic.

Throughout history, speeches have inspired social change, which has affected future generations and sometimes changed the course of history.

All speeches seek to persuade, inform, inspire or entertain their audience. A great speech achieves its purpose, keeps the audience interested and leaves a lasting impact.

These public figures have all given powerful speeches that have made an impact.

Mahatma Gandhi

Greta Thunberg

Understanding a Speech

To understand a speech and the impact it has, you must understand more than the words. Consider the following questions:

Speaker Who is giving the speech?

What do we know about the person giving the speech?

Background What was happening in society when the speech was delivered?

Knowing what was happening to people at the time the speech was given helps us understand why it was delivered and its importance.

Audience Where was the speech delivered and to whom?

When giving a speech it's important to make it suitable for who you are speaking to. The audience needs to be able to relate to it.

Amanda Gorman

Kevin Rudd

Purpose What was the speech trying to achieve?

The purpose of a speech relates to its background and audience.

Theme What is the main idea in the speech?

The speeches in this book may seem unrelated, but they all share one common theme: hope for the future. Even Greta Thunberg's angry speech finishes with "change is coming ...". A speech might have several smaller themes as well.

Tone What emotions did the speech inspire?

Speeches are delivered with a specific **tone**. For example, using words related to battle inspires a fighting spirit in the audience.

Literary device What techniques were used to try to persuade the audience?

A literary device is a technique the speaker uses that allows them to convey a deeper meaning. Speeches use literary devices for impact. A speaker will use many literary devices within one speech. Common examples include repetition, personification, inclusive pronouns and asking rhetorical questions. There are more than 100 literary devices.

Reaction How did the speech affect the audience?

Did the speech successfully persuade the audience to agree with the speaker? Did it inspire them? Or did it turn the audience against the speaker?

Legacy How is the speech still relevant today?

What was the lasting impact of the speech?

FREEDOM OR DEATH

Emmeline Pankhurst (1913)

Speaker

Emmeline Pankhurst was an English **suffragette**. She believed that women needed the right to vote before their living conditions could improve. Her **campaign** for women's rights was known around the world.

Background

In the early twentieth century, the only countries in which women had **suffrage** (the right to vote) were Aotearoa New Zealand, Australia (excluding First Nations women) and Finland. Many men were opposed to women's suffrage, so the suffragettes had to fight hard. They went on hunger strikes, had **rallies**, chained themselves to buildings, fought with police and burnt buildings to get people's attention.

Audience

In 1913, Pankhurst travelled to the USA and delivered her "Freedom or Death" speech to an enthusiastic crowd of mostly women.

Purpose

Pankhurst's purpose in travelling to the USA was to raise support, awareness and money for her campaign. Her theme was that women were soldiers fighting for their right to vote. Her tone was serious and determined.

Quote

> Either women are to be killed or women are to have the vote.

Literary device

Pankhurst used words connected to the army or military to illustrate that the suffragettes were fighting for their cause: "I am here as a soldier who has temporarily left the field of battle in order to explain – it seems strange it should have to be explained – what civil war is like when civil war is waged by women." It aimed to make the audience feel courageous and encourage them to join the fight.

Suffragettes protest in London in 1912.

Reaction

Some people criticised Pankhurst for her combative attitude. However, this speech energised the women's movement of the early 1900s in both the United Kingdom and the USA.

Relevance

This speech reminds us of how difficult it was for women to get the vote.

When Women Were First Granted National Suffrage at National Level

Country	Year
Aotearoa New Zealand	→ 1893
Australia	→ 1902 (non-First Nations) → 1962 (First Nations)
Finland	→ 1906
Denmark	→ 1915
Russia	→ 1917
Canada	→ 1917 (mostly) → 1960 (Indigenous)
United Kingdom	→ 1918 (partial) → 1928 (full)
Sweden	→ 1919
USA	→ 1920 (mostly) → 1960 (Black women in Southern states)
South Africa	→ 1930 (European and Asian women) → 1994 (all women)
China	→ 1949

People gather at the headquarters of the Women's Suffrage Party of Manhattan in New York.

“QUIT INDIA

Mahatma Gandhi (1942)

Speaker

Mahatma Gandhi was an Indian lawyer and political leader who fought for independence for India. He led major protests and worked hard for equality and justice for all people.

Background

In the early twentieth century, the British ruled over India and most Indians were strongly against it. In 1930, Gandhi gained worldwide attention when he led a 24-day march **protesting** British taxes imposed on Indians. Gandhi urged Indians to stop buying British-made items, and to not cooperate with or work for the British.

Audience

On 8 August 1942, Gandhi gave three “Quit India” speeches: one to the All India Congress Committee; one to Hindu and Muslim Indians and government servants; and one to the British Government.

Purpose

All three speeches had the theme of Indian self-rule. The tone of the speeches was formal, **logical** and peaceful.

Quote

We shall either free India or die in the attempt ...

Literary device

Gandhi uses an **oxymoron** in his speech: "a non-violent soldier". A soldier's actions can be violent, so these words don't usually go together. This communicates **irony** and makes the audience think.

Reaction

Gandhi, his wife Kasturba and other Indian leaders were jailed by the British within a day of the speech. "Do or Die" became the unifying slogan for Gandhi's followers across India. Gandhi's wife died in prison.

Relevance

Gandhi's "Quit India" speech remains relevant today as an example of the power of **unity** in the face of **oppression**. It is a reminder of the sacrifices people made fighting for India's independence.

People in India celebrate Independence Day.

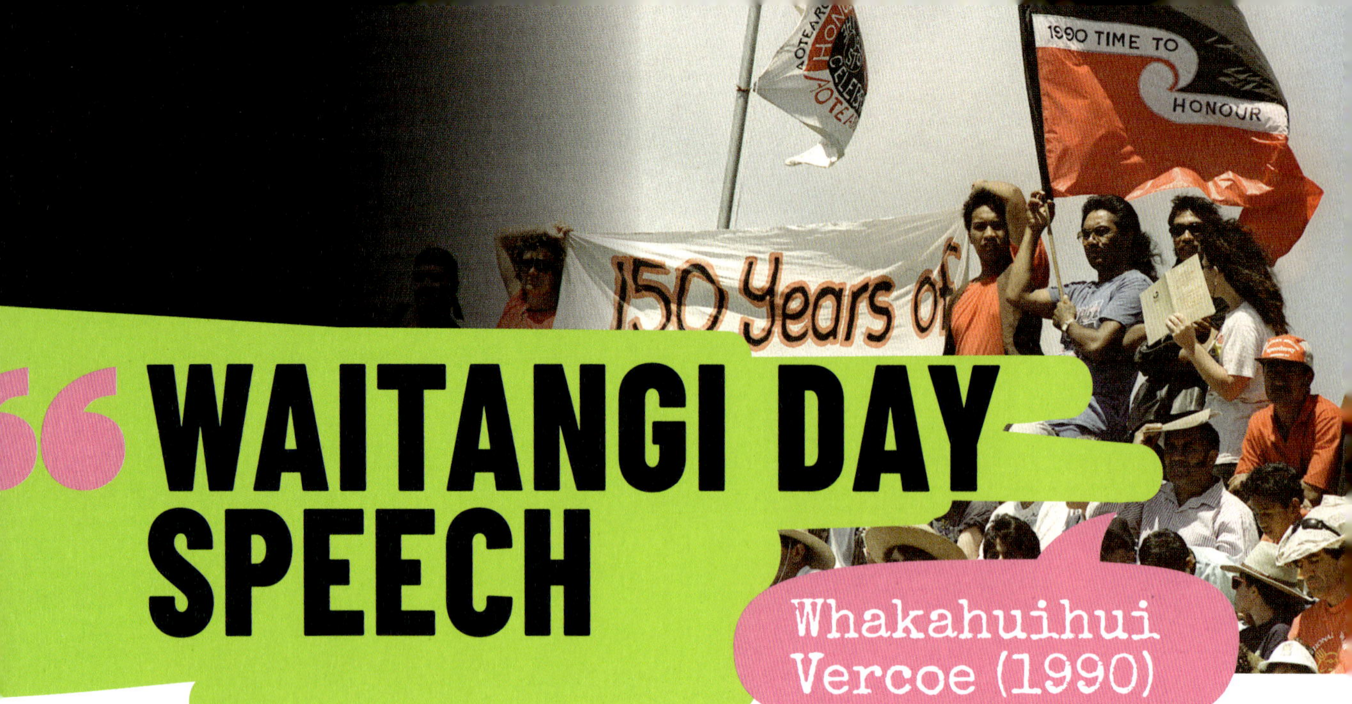

WAITANGI DAY SPEECH

Whakahuihui Vercoe (1990)

Speaker

Whakahuihui Vercoe, the Anglican Bishop of Aotearoa New Zealand, who was of both British and Māori descent, gave the Waitangi Day speech in 1990. He was upset at how many Māori were living in poor conditions, and he felt he needed to say something.

Background

Every year on 6 February, New Zealanders **commemorate** the signing of their founding document, the **Treaty** of Waitangi. The Treaty is an agreement that was made between the British Crown and Māori in 1840. In 1990, the 150th anniversary of the Treaty was a huge celebration. However, some Māori felt the Treaty promises had been broken and were protesting this celebration.

Audience

The speech was made at the Waitangi Treaty Grounds, in front of Queen Elizabeth II, many dignitaries and a crowd of thousands.

Purpose

Because the speech was impromptu (made up on the spot), there was no written text. Bishop Vercoe suggested that the government had failed to honour the Treaty and had marginalised Māori people.

Quote

> You have not honoured the Treaty.

Literary device

Bishop Vercoe addressed Queen Elizabeth II directly, making the relationship between the Crown and the Māori people more personal. He also used a first-person point of view – "I have come … I cry …" – to create an emotional connection.

Whakahuihui Vercoe appealed to Queen Elizabeth II in his Waitangi Day speech.

Reaction

When Bishop Vercoe finished his speech, everyone sat silently. People were shocked that Bishop Vercoe could be so **discourteous** to the British Queen. However, there was support from the Māori people.

Relevance

The Waitangi Day speech gave Māori people hope for a more equitable future.

THE NATIONAL APOLOGY

Kevin Rudd (2008)

Speaker

Kevin Rudd was the Prime Minister of Australia from 2007 to 2010 and June to September 2013.

Background

A 1997 report recommended the Australian Government offer an official apology to First Nations Australians for past government actions. Between 1910 and the 1970s, many First Nations children were forcibly removed from their families. These children are known as the Stolen Generations. The Prime Minister at the time, John Howard, refused to issue an apology. Eleven years later, the Labor Prime Minister Kevin Rudd gave a formal national apology to Australia's First Nations peoples.

Audience

The speech was given in Parliament on 13 February 2008 and was watched on TV by millions of people throughout Australia.

Purpose

The speech is formal and apologetic. It refers to the past, the present and the future of Australia.

Quote

> We apologise for the laws and policies of successive Parliaments and governments that have inflicted profound grief, suffering and loss on these our fellow Australians.

Literary device

Repetition of phrases, including “we reflect”, ”we apologise” and “we say sorry”, helps the audience to understand and remember a specific message.

Reaction

The Prime Minister’s speech was met with applause, tears and relief from many First Nations peoples. However, some members of the Opposition disagreed with the apology and walked out of Parliament in protest.

People gather in Canberra to hear Kevin Rudd deliver the National Apology in 2008.

Relevance

After Rudd’s National Apology, many First Nations peoples felt heard and validated.

THE MISOGYNY SPEECH

Julia Gillard (2012)

Speaker

Julia Gillard was Australia's first female Prime Minister, from 2010 to 2013. Over the months leading up to the Misogyny Speech, Gillard had been criticised by the Leader of the Opposition, Tony Abbott, who accused her of **sexism**.

Background

In the early twenty-first century, women in the Australian Parliament felt badly treated by some of their colleagues. The media and some male politicians made negative personal remarks about female politicians, especially if they were unmarried or had no children. This is known as misogyny, which is a dislike of or prejudice against women.

Audience

The speech was given in Parliament to Gillard's own Labor Party, the Opposition and press reporters.

Purpose

Gillard's speech was an impromptu **rebuttal** to Abbott's criticism of her. It was emotional and powerful.

Tony Abbott speaks as the Leader of the Opposition in 2012.

Quote

> I will not be lectured about sexism and misogyny by this man. Not now. Not ever.

Literary device

By addressing Tony Abbott as the "Leader of the Opposition" in her speech, Gillard took away his personal identity and left him just with a label. This act showed her dominance, power and **hierarchy** in Parliament.

Reaction

The Misogyny Speech became one of the most memorable speeches ever given in the Australian Parliament. It was adapted into a song sung by the Australian Voices choir, and in 2020 it was voted the most unforgettable moment in Australian TV history.

Relevance

This speech raised awareness about the sexist and misogynistic treatment of women by men in Australian society. Some women now feel more confident to speak out against similar treatment in their own workplaces.

“OUR WORDS CAN CHANGE THE WHOLE WORLD

Malala Yousafzai (2013)

Speaker

Malala Yousafzai is an education **activist**. At age 15, while living in her home country of Pakistan, she was shot in the head by a Taliban gunman trying to stop her activism.

Background

In Pakistan, the Taliban (a **repressive** religious group) banned girls from going to school. They used violence and intimidation to control people. After the assassination attempt, Malala was flown to Germany and then England to be cared for and receive ongoing treatment for her injuries.

Audience

When Malala had recovered from her injuries, she gave this speech at the **United Nations** Assembly in New York on her 16th birthday (12 July 2013).

Purpose

Malala gave a persuasive speech promoting the reasons why education is necessary for children.

Malala fought for girls in Pakistan to be able to go to school.

Quote

> Education is the only solution.

Literary device

Malala referenced important religious leaders (Muhammad, Jesus Christ, Lord Buddha), activists (Nelson Mandela, Mahatma Gandhi, Bacha Khan, Mother Teresa), and her parents in her speech. This appealed to a broad audience.

Reaction

- 12 July is known around the world as Malala Day.
- The speech was given the title "Speak Out", set to music and performed by the BBC National Orchestra on International Women's Day in 2017.
- In 2014, at the age of 17, Malala won the Nobel Peace Prize.

Relevance

Using the slogan "I am Malala", a petition was formed demanding that there be no child left out of school by 2015. Unfortunately, this petition has not yet been successful but is still in progress.

MESSAGE OF PEACE

Jane Goodall (2017)

Speaker

Dame Jane Goodall is a British **primatologist** and **anthropologist** known for researching wild chimpanzees in Tanzania.

Background

The United Nations General Assembly selects distinguished individuals from around the world to become UN Messengers of Peace. As a Messenger of Peace, Goodall volunteers her time and passion to raise awareness of the UN efforts to improve the lives of people around the world.

Audience

On 16 September 2017, Goodall spoke to students at the annual UN International Day of Peace in New York. Her audience was mainly teenagers from around the world.

Purpose

The purpose of this speech was to raise awareness of the United Nations' efforts to secure world peace. Goodall spoke in a clear, calm and logical manner. She remained seated and spoke conversationally.

Quote

> Each and every one of us makes some impact on the planet every single day that we live ... how will those little choices affect future generations?

Literary device

Goodall asked questions and gave possible solutions to persuade the audience that her ideas were answers to a problem. Her questions contained pronouns like "we", "us" and "our" to make the audience feel included. *What can we do? How do you find peace within yourself? What do we buy?*

Jane Goodall works with chimpanzees in Tanzania in 1965.

Reaction

In 2019, Goodall was named by *Time Magazine* as one of the 100 most influential people in the world.

Relevance

We haven't yet achieved world peace, and Goodall's message, with its practical ideas, is still relevant.

"YOU STOLE MY CHILDHOOD

Greta Thunberg (2019)

Speaker

On 20 September 2019, Greta Thunberg led the biggest climate-change protest in history with 6 million people across 150 countries. Three days later, she spoke at the United Nations Climate Action Summit in New York.

Background

The Paris Agreement is an international treaty on climate change that was agreed to by many countries in 2015. Sweden did not comply with some of the climate-change actions. A Swedish teenager gained worldwide attention by protesting daily outside the Swedish Parliament, refusing to attend school until her government acted on climate change. That teenager was Greta Thunberg.

Audience

The audience consisted of assembled world leaders, politicians and media, and was broadcast around the world. She began with a message for world leaders: "... we'll be watching you".

Purpose

Thunberg's speech was about climate change. Her purpose was to make world leaders change the rules in their countries, so that actions that contribute to climate change are reduced.

Quote

> You have stolen my dreams
> and my childhood
> with your empty words ...
> we will not let you
> get away with this ...

Greta Thunberg leads a climate protest in Bristol, UK, in 2020.

Literary device

Thunberg was a teenager speaking to the world's most powerful adults. She was passionate and angry, and she spoke from the heart. This type of free speech from an ordinary person to someone of high political power is known as **parrhesia**. The person talking is risking anger and punishment to convey an uncomfortable truth.

Reaction

Thunberg's blunt speech was ridiculed and dismissed by some leaders. Others were impressed and inspired. She became a household name around the world.

Relevance

Thunberg's message is still relevant because, despite her warnings, global warming continues to increase.

THE HILL WE CLIMB

Amanda Gorman (2021)

Speaker

Amanda Gorman, a 22-year-old American poet and activist, performed her poem *The Hill We Climb* at the **inauguration** of American President Joe Biden.

Background

The inauguration of Joe Biden as the 46th president of the United States took place on 20 January 2021, against a background of the Covid-19 pandemic and people protesting.

Audience

Gorman performed her poem to former presidents and vice presidents, ambassadors, judges and other dignitaries. It was also televised around the world.

Purpose

The Hill We Climb is an "occasional poem", which is a poem written to celebrate a special occasion. Its tone was hopeful and optimistic.

Literary device

Gorman used her voice, phrasing, hand gestures and facial expressions to emphasise important ideas. She also used end rhyme (a rhyme in the last syllables of two or more lines) to create a sense of rhythm.

Reaction

Gorman gained immediate fame on social media because of the way she used the modern style of **spoken-word** poetry to deliver the poem's message.

Relevance

The Hill We Climb contains themes of hope, healing and unity. These themes are as relevant today as they were in 2021.

Amanda Gorman speaks at the 2024 Democratic National Convention in Chicago, USA.

COMPARE AND CONTRAST

Inspirational speeches give us hope, **optimism** and a drive to make positive change. Every speech is unique and created in a specific time and place in history. By comparing (noticing similarities) and contrasting (noticing differences) between speeches, you can decide what you think makes a great speech.

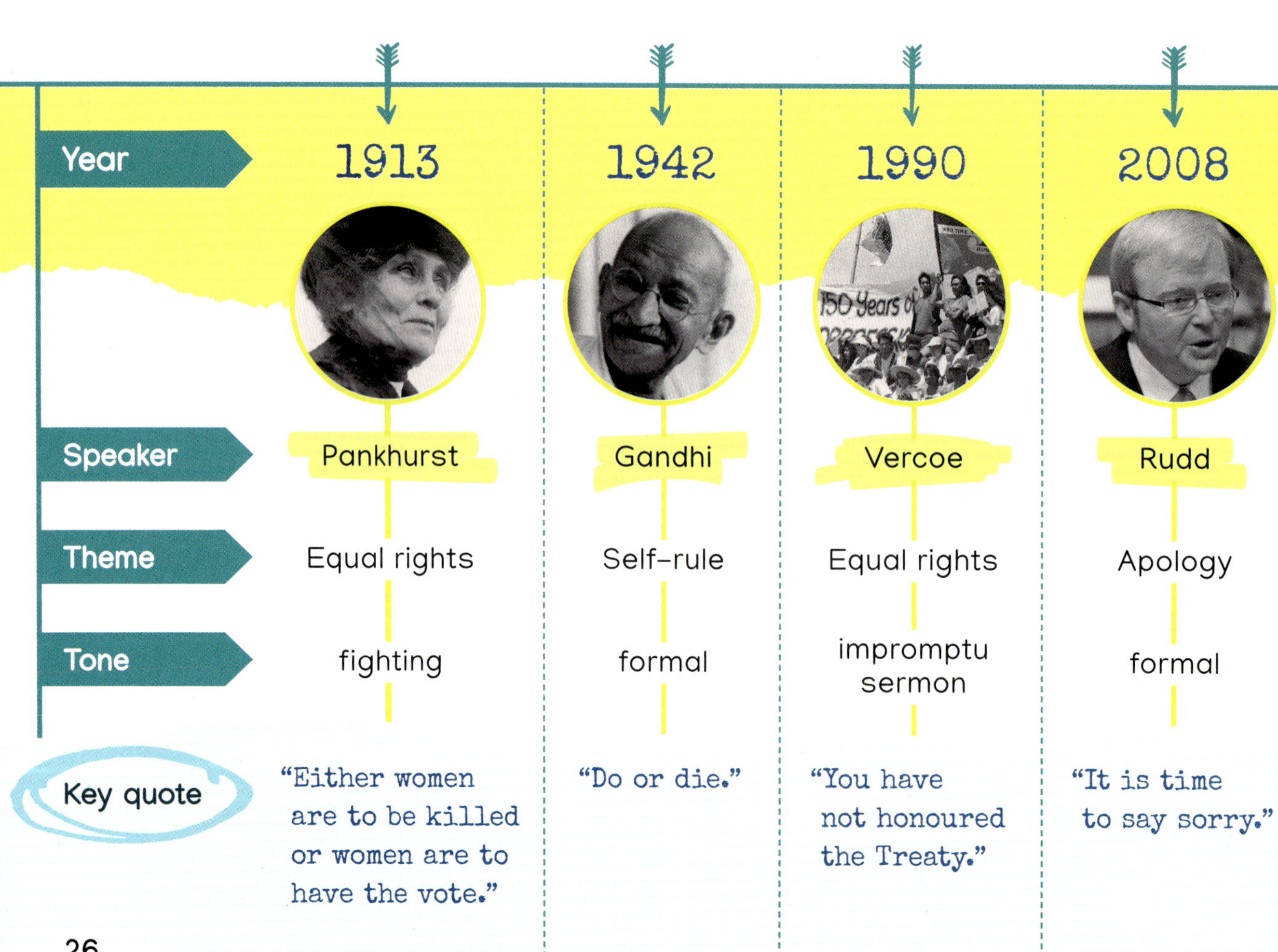

Year	1913	1942	1990	2008
Speaker	Pankhurst	Gandhi	Vercoe	Rudd
Theme	Equal rights	Self-rule	Equal rights	Apology
Tone	fighting	formal	impromptu sermon	formal
Key quote	"Either women are to be killed or women are to have the vote."	"Do or die."	"You have not honoured the Treaty."	"It is time to say sorry."

Malala Yousafzai is awarded honorary Canadian citizenship by Prime Minister Justin Trudeau in 2017.
2012
Gillard
Misogyny
rebuttal
"Not now. Not ever."
2013
Yousafzai
Education
persuasive
"Education is the only solution."
2017
Goodall
Peace
conversational
"Every one of us makes some impact on the planet."
2019
Thunberg
Environmentalism
angry
"You have stolen my childhood."
2021
Gorman
Future peace
poetic

MY FAVOURITE SPEECH

Choose a speech that resonates with you. It might be a speech from this book, a poem or a play. It might be given by a politician, a celebrity, a comedian, a person in history, an actor, a talking animal or even an animated character.

- Why do you like this speech?
- What is the message?
- Who is the audience?
- What message does the speaker hope to send with their speech?
- What are some literary devices the speaker uses?
- What is a memorable quote?
- Who might not like this speech?
- Is the speech relevant today?

Singer Lady Gaga gives a speech after accepting the Artists Inspiration Award in 2018.

Barack Obama gave many speeches during his time as US President.

HOW TO WRITE A SPEECH

Writing a speech is easy if you break it down into different parts.

Topic

Choose a subject that is important to you:

Theme

What is the main message you want to express? A speech about history could have many different themes. For example: war, politics, peace or influential leaders.

Purpose

1. An informative speech teaches people about a topic.
2. An entertaining speech amuses people.
3. A persuasive speech convinces people of a particular viewpoint.

Audience

Who is your audience? How will you make your speech suitable to teach/entertain/persuade them? How will you get and keep their attention?

Introduction

- Introduce yourself and your topic.
- Explain why people should listen to you.
- Outline what you will be talking about.

Body

- Introduce and explain each of your main points in order.
- Use literary devices to give your speech more impact.

Conclusion

- Summarise what you said.
- End with a strong final sentence. This aims to leave your audience thinking about what you have said in your speech.

Delivery

- Talk clearly and confidently.
- Vary your voice, facial expressions and body language.
- Make eye contact.
- Repeat your key message.

Rehearse

Practise your speech with another person or record yourself and then play it back. This will help you feel confident.

Glossary

activist (*noun*)	a person who works to achieve political or social change
anthropologist (*noun*)	a person who studies the human race
campaign (*noun*)	a series of activities intended to achieve a social or political aim
commemorate (*verb*)	to remind people of an important event or person from the past
discourteous (*adjective*)	having bad manners and not respecting other people
hierarchy (*noun*)	a system in society in which people are organised by importance
inauguration (*noun*)	a special ceremony at which a new public leader is introduced
irony (*noun*)	a funny or strange aspect of a situation that is different from what you expect
logical (*adjective*)	seeming natural, reasonable or sensible
oppression (*noun*)	cruel and unfair treatment of people, especially by not giving them the same rights as other people
optimism (*noun*)	a feeling that good things will happen
oxymoron (*noun*)	a phrase that uses two words that seem to be the opposite of each other
parrhesia (*noun*)	boldness or freedom of speech
primatologist (*noun*)	a scientist who studies the biology of non-human primates
protesting (*verb*)	to say or do something to show that you disagree with something
rallies (*noun*)	large public meetings, especially those held to support an idea or political party
rebuttal (*noun*)	the act of saying or proving that a statement is false
repressive (*adjective*)	controlling people by force and limiting their freedom
sexism (*noun*)	the unfair treatment of people, particularly women, because of their gender

spoken-word (*adjective*) — a type of poetry that is spoken aloud to an audience

suffrage (*noun*) — the right to vote in political elections

suffragette (*noun*) — a member of a group of women who helped women win the right to vote in political elections

tone (*noun*) — the quality of someone's voice, especially when expressing a particular emotion

treaty (*noun*) — an agreement between two or more countries

United Nations (*noun*) — an association of many countries that aims to improve and solve political problems in the world in a peaceful way

unity (*noun*) — the state of being in agreement and working together

Index